THE BUMPER QUIZ BOOK

compiled by Michael Holt

illustrated by Chris Winn

A Hippo Book
Scholastic Publications Limited
London

Scholastic Publications Ltd,
161 Fulham Road, London SW3 6SW England

Scholastic Book Services,
50 West 44th Street, New York 10036 NY USA

Scholastic Tab Publications Ltd,
123 Newkirk Road, Richmond Hill, Ontario L4C 3G5
Canada

H J Ashton Co Pty Ltd, Box 579,
Gosford, New South Wales, Australia

H J Ashton Co Pty Ltd,
9-11 Fairfax Avenue, Penrose, Auckland, New Zealand

First published by Scholastic Publications Ltd 1981
Copyright © Michael Holt 1981
Illustrations Copyright © Chris Winn 1981
All rights reserved

Typeset by Input Typesetting Ltd.
Printed and bound in Great Britain by
Cox & Wyman Ltd, Reading

This book is sold subject to the condition that it shall not, by way
of trade or otherwise, be lent, re-sold, hired out, or otherwise
circulated without the publisher's prior consent in any form of
binding or cover other than that in which it is published and
without a similar condition including this condition being
imposed on the subsequent purchaser.

The Bumper Quiz Book

How can you make four triangles from six matches?

What is a horse's frog?

Which insect lives underground for seventeen years?

What do you get if you divide four by a half and add two?

Serena Dippity, her dog Smiler, and Magico the magician introduce you to over 230 brand-new brain-teasers.

Stretch your mind around crosswords, cross-sums and laddergrams. Test your general knowledge - what do you know about nature, history, books, geography, science, inventors, dinosaurs, music and numbers? Learn how to do illusions and find out some fascinating facts. You'll find hours of fun in this cram-packed bumper book.

Michael Holt was once an actor, but he has written over a hundred books and even appeared on his own 'Mathemagical' show on BBC television. Apart from inventing new puzzles for his books he spends some of his time visiting schools to show children that maths can be fun!

Introduction

Meet two rather special people and a dog:
Magico, the celebrated wizard of prestidigitation
(sleight of hand, that is), Serena Dippity, a scatty
young lady, and her long-suffering but faithful
foxy hound Smiler. How did I come upon them?
Well, one winter's morning as I sat down to
write this book the picture of a pretty village
nestling in rolling countryside, rather like the
village where I live, came into my mind. Along
the lane came Serena, with Smiler trotting at her
back wheel. As she cycled past one of the
cottages she spied through the hollyhocks the
strangest inhabitant of all, Magico, the kindly
magician. They seemed to me to be just the kind
of people who would enjoy living in puzzleland!
Serena's name, as you may have guessed, comes
from the old-fashioned word *serendipity*, which
means the "ability to make happy chance finds"
– which I hope is what the book will bring you.
As for Smiler, I'm very fond of dogs – I have a
faithful one myself, called Mollie, though she's
not much good at puzzles. And Magico – well I
do a mathemagical show now and then for
children, sometimes on television.

And where did the quizzes come from? Many

of them come from questions I have been asked and some are the sort of quiz I liked when I was a child. So there are quizzes on every possible subject, from witches to fairy tales, horses to insects, about famous people in history and strange places in geography.

I hope you have as much fun trying to answer the quizzes and solve the puzzles as I had in making them up!

THE BUMPER QUIZ BOOK

The Camford Cottages Puzzle

1 The picture shows Camford, the village where Serena Dippity lives with her dog, Smiler.

Serena and Smiler live here

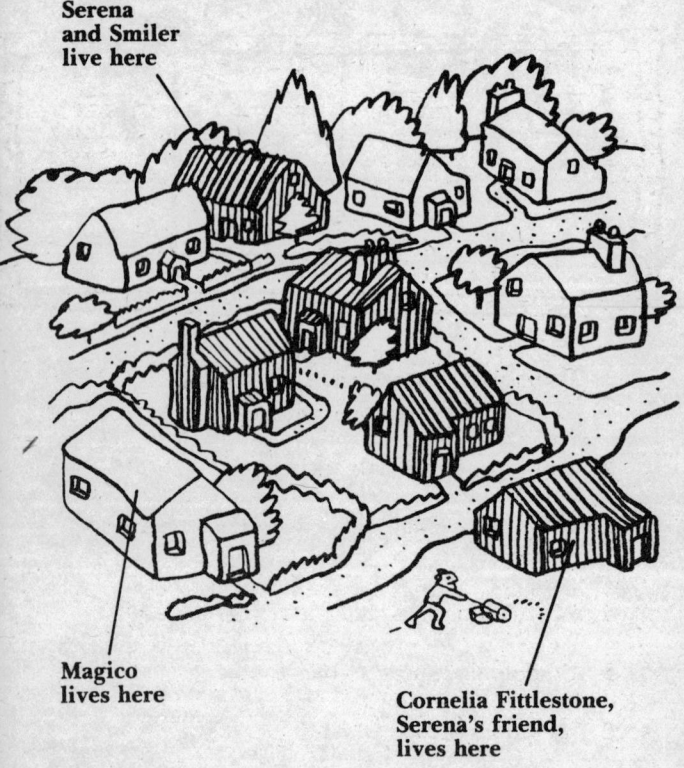

Magico lives here

Cornelia Fittlestone, Serena's friend, lives here

Some of the cottages have chimneys and some have not; some are white and some are black, as you can see. The puzzle is, can you work out how many of each kind there are in the village? What you've got to do is put your answers in the special table Serena has drawn for you.

She's begun it for you by counting three white cottages with no chimney.

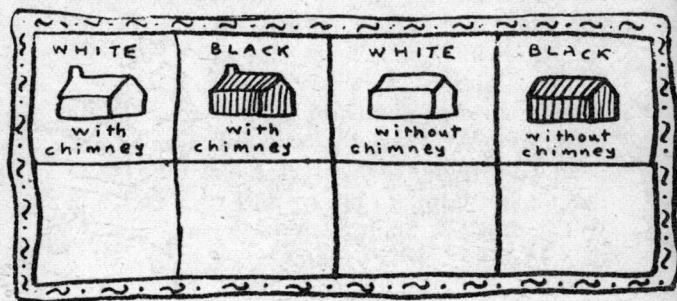

Dolphins, Boops and Clicks

2 Can any sea animals speak?

3 What sea animal makes a noise like clanking chains?

4 Why do dolphins make a "click" sound?

5 Do dolphins speak to one another?

6 How do dolphins whistle?

7 How many "words" can a dolphin speak?

8 What does a dolphin's voice sound like?

Summer Hols Puzzle

9 Serena Dippity was planning her summer holiday. She had the holiday brochures spread out on the table before her. "Where shall we go?" she asked Smiler, her dog. He cocked an ear. "Funville?" she suggested, patting him fondly. "But look, it says here, if you travel through an even number of stations your dog can travel free. We'll take the train from Camford. So what's our route? It says there's only one. We don't count Camford but we do Funville. Can you work it out, Smiler?"

Can you find Serena's route?

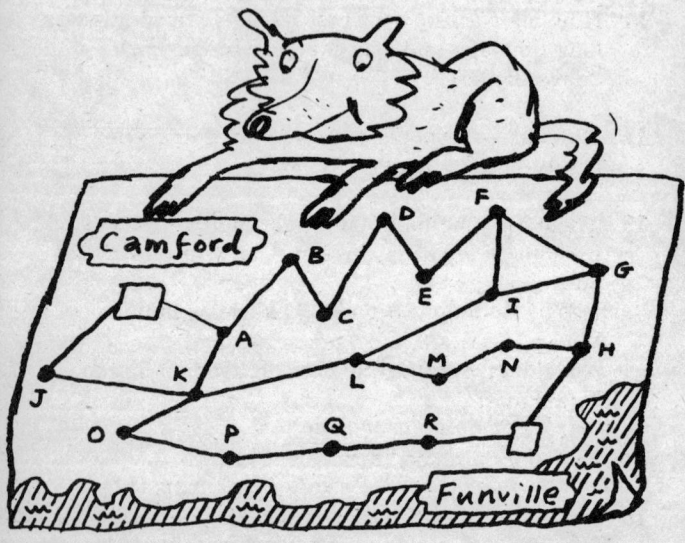

Horse Sense

10 You measure the height of a horse or pony in hands. Can you say how much a hand is?

11 How big was the very first horse? It lived a long, long time ago and was called Eohippus, or "dawn horse".

12 How tall is a Shetland pony? Can you say in hands or centimetres?

13 There are nine mountain and moorland breeds of pony to be found in this list. Can you pick them out?
Dale, Palomino, Shetland, Dartmoor, Hunter, Welsh Mountain, Hackney, Highland, Appaloosa, Fell, Connemara, Exmoor, Morgan, New Forest.

14 Why does a horse "flick" its skin?

15 What part of our body is a horse's hoof like – our finger, our foot or our nails?

16 What is a horse's frog?

17 What is a horse's frog *for*?

18 How do you tell a horse's age?

Serena's Dippy Postcard

19 Serena dashed off a postcard to her dizzy chum
Cornelia Fittlestone. It simply said:
COME TO TEA NEXT THURSDAY. IF YOU
DON'T GET THIS POSTCARD, LET ME
KNOW AT ONCE!
What was dippy about her postcard message?

Magico's matches

20 Take six matches. How can you make four
triangles out of them? Each triangle must be
made up of three matches and no matches may
cross over each other.
Hint: Make a tetrahedron . . . if that's any help
to you!

It happened Yesterday

21 Who was Queen Boudicca and when did she
live?

22 Which Queen of England had the longest reign?

23 Who was the Prime Minister of England at the
end of Queen Victoria's reign? Hint: He liked
daffodils, and Queen Victoria called him
"Dizzie" for short.

24 What happened at Sarajevo when Archduke Ferdinand was shot there? Hint: It started a war.

25 Who was the first man to discover the West Indies? Vasco da Gama, Magellan, Columbus, Drake, Raleigh.

26 Who brought the potato to Europe? And when did he do it?

27 What was the Charge of the Light Brigade?

28 Who painted the *Mona Lisa*? And what is the other name of this painting?

29 Where was Cathay?

30 What was the "year of confusion"? Clue: It was in Roman times and lasted 445 days!

31 Who demanded "Give us back our eleven days"? And when did they make the demand?

32 Which King Edward of England was the youngest monarch to come to the throne, and which reigned the shortest time?

33 Can you name King Henry VIII's six wives and say what befell each of them? Clue: divorced, beheaded, died, divorced, beheaded, survived.

34 Who said "There is time to finish the game and beat the Armada too!"? And what was the game he was playing?

The Case of the Stolen Flute

35 Serena, who as you know teaches music, was cycling back through Camford one evening after giving a flute lesson to her friend Cornelia Fittlestone. Smiler was trotting quietly behind her. Suddenly she was waved down by a torch held by Constable Dimwitty, who was nothing if not zealous.

"What 'ave you got in that basket?" he demanded.

"My flute and music," she replied sweetly.

"And 'ow do I know you 'aven't stolen them?" he asked cunningly. "I think you 'ad better accompany me to the Station and explain everything to the H'inspector."

At the Police Station the constable explained why he had arrested Serena Dippity to a tired Inspector Groan. "Tell me, Miss Dippity," sighed the Inspector who was used to this sort of thing, "Did you steal the flute and music?" Serena gave the Inspector a dazzling smile and opened her blue eyes wide.

"Well, Inspector, if I'm not innocent, my name's not Serena Dippity! Cross my heart." Smiler woofed assent.

"That settles it then," said the Inspector. "All right Constable, you can escort Miss Dippity to her cottage. Good night, Miss Dippity. I'm sorry you've been troubled."

Can you tell by *logical* reasoning how the Inspector knew she was innocent? You can take it that what she said to him was true.

36 Disc-o Puzzle

Try this. Fill in the discs with the numbers 2, 3, 4, 5, 6, 7, 8 so that each row of discs adds up to the same number, 15.

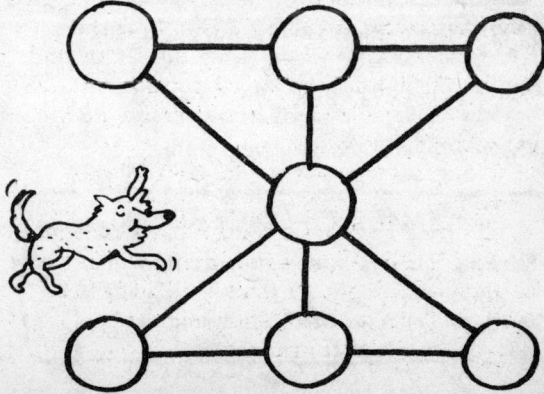

Sock Pairs

37 Serena was off to the local disco one evening. She had just opened a drawerful of her electric red, blue and gold socks when her bedroom light fused. She had to find a matching pair in the dark. How many did she need to take into the light to make sure she had a matching pair? The fewest number, of course!

Money makes the World go Round

38 What is wampum?

39 What is Maundy money?

40 What is blood money?

41 Where are sweets still used as money?

42 When was tobacco used as money?

43 What is the oldest coin used as money?

44 What is the earliest silver coin ever used?

45 What is the oldest paper money note?

46 Why do "silver" coins have a milled edge?

SMILER'S ONCERS

Serena: There's a man downstairs with a funny face.
Smiler: Tell him we've got one!

Eggsactly!

47 Serena Dippity had three number four eggs and one lighter one, but they all looked exactly alike, and she wanted to find out which was the lighter egg. She had scale pans. How did she find out which was the lighter egg in just two weighings? She marked the eggs **a**, **b**, **c**, **d**.

The Crossed Coins Puzzle

48 Here are six coins arranged as a cross.

The puzzle is this. Can you move one coin only to make a cross with *four* coins along both arms of the cross?

The Alarm-clock Puzzle

49 Dog-tired, Smiler settled down in his basket for the night and Serena decided to turn in early, at 8 o'clock. She set her alarm clock for 9 o'clock the next morning. When the alarm woke them, how long had they both been asleep?

SMILER'S ONCERS

Smiler: "When is a candle not a candle?"
Answer: When it's a-light!

Witches, Monsters and Folklore

50 What was a witch's familiar?
Her hat, her cat, her broom, or her magic?

51 Who was the Witch of Endor?

52 What is a warlock?

53 What is the Loch Ness Monster?

54 Who was Rip Van Winkle?

55 Who was the Wizard of Oz?

56 What was the Centaur?

57 Who were Castor and Pollux?

58 Who were Romulus and Remus?

59 Who had writhing snakes on her head instead of hair?

60 Who killed Medusa and how did he do it?

61 Smiler's Pills
Because Smiler wasn't too well, Serena went to the vet who gave her four pills to make him better. When Serena got home she read the label on the box to Smiler: "It says 'Take one every hour'." Now, how long did the pills last, do you think?

62 How's your Division?

Divide four by a half and then add two.
What's the answer?

What Do you Know?

63 What is Venus's fly-trap, and what does it trap?

64 What is the oldest surviving kind of tree?

65 What is the tallest tree in the world?

66 Who first flew the English Channel in a powered airplane?

67 Which woman first flew from England to Australia?

68 Who was General Tom Thumb?

69 What is the largest diamond ever discovered?

70 What is the Plimsoll line – shown here? And what do the letters on it mean?

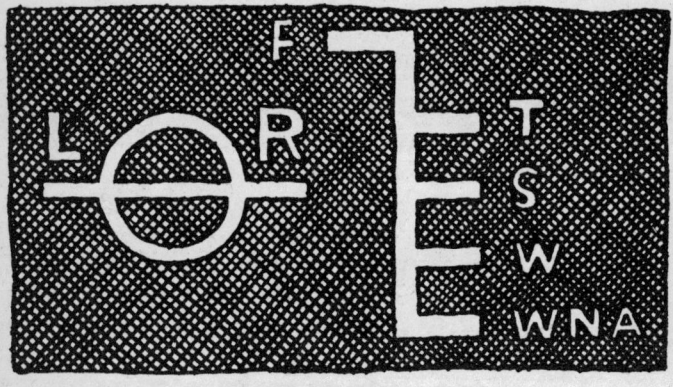

71 What is an aqueduct?

72 What is a cobza?

73 There have been several different keyed musical instruments all played like the piano. Here are five of them: spinet, clavichord, piano, virginal, harpsichord.
Can you put the right name to each instrument shown here?

74 This is a picture of an abacus. What is it used for?

75 Where did the Romans get the purple colour for their togas?

76 For what things would you find these names used:
Achief, Nebuly, Dancetty, Reguly, Francy
Are they flags, shields or medals?

77 How can you tell the age of a fish?

78 Serena was busy buying something for the house. Stamped on it she found these signs. Do you know what they are?

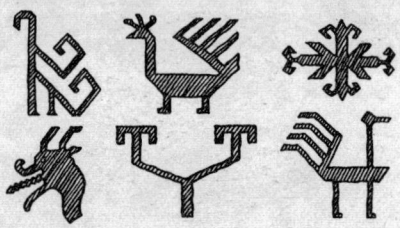

Clue: You can fly on a magic one.

79 How can Serena bake some potatoes in her oven double-quick?

Magico's hat illusion

80 Magico, the great illusionist, has just pulled a rabbit out of his top hat. Well, that's one illusion, for sure. But there's another one to be seen if you look carefully. Which do you think is bigger – the brim or the height of Magico's top hat?

You'd better measure it to make sure your eyes aren't fooling you!

Magico's Magic Knot

81 Magico has found a way to make a knot in a
strip of paper simply by cutting it with a pair of
scissors! This is what you do. Take a long strip
of paper. Hold the two ends in your hands in
order to join them. But before you do, give one
end two full twists and an extra half twist; then
glue them or join them with tape. Now you are
ready for the great trick. Cut the joined strip all
the way along its middle. When you have
finished will you find that you have. . . two
separate rings or one whole ring and something
else?

Know Your Cats and Dogs

82 Why do dogs turn round and round in their
baskets before going to sleep?

83 Why do dogs pant?

84 Why does your dog jump up to greet you when
you get back home?

85 What sort of sounds can a dog hear?

86 How do shepherds talk to their sheepdogs?

87 Why do cats claw curtains?

88 Can cats see in the dark?

89 There are nine breeds of domestic cat to be picked out in this list. The others are wild cats. Can you spot them?
Silver Tabby, Lion, Abyssinian, Manx, Puma, Siamese, Burman, Civet, Lynx, Japanese Kimona, Ocelot, Maltese, Persian, Angora, Tiger.

90 What sort of thing are all these names for?
Weimaraner, Schipperke, Puli, Maltese, Mexican Hairless, Dandie Dinmont, Viszla, Griffon.

91 Noughts'n Crosses

Serena is playing noughts and crosses with Smiler. It is Smiler's turn to put his X down. Where must he put it to stop Serena (O) from winning?

Magic Nine Times Circle

92 Serena was trying to teach Smiler his nine times table while they were playing on the beach last year.

"Nine ones are nine, nine twos are. . . ?"
She prompted.

"Eighty-one," growled Smiler, none too happy with this "game".

"No, no, Smiler. You've got it back to front. It's eighteen, not eighty-one."
Then she had a brainwave. She took a stick and drew a circle in the sand.
Smiler cocked his head appreciatively as she placed eight pebbles round the circle's edge then numbered them 2 to 9.
Then she scratched the numbers 1 to 8 inside the circle, as shown here:

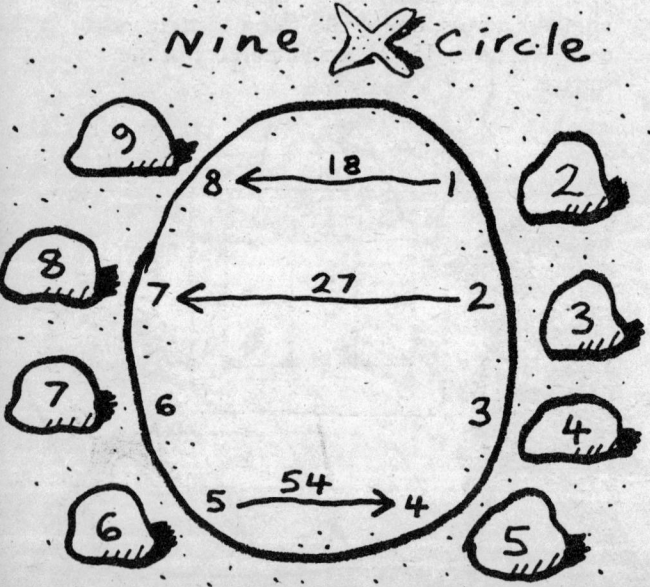

"Now Smiler, let's begin again," she said brightly. For 2 times 9 she drew a line from stone 2 and joined the 1 straight across to the 8. She read off the answer "one-eight or eighteen."
For 3 times 9 she drew a line from stone 3 to join the 2 to the 7 and read the answer "two-seven or twenty-seven."
And for 6 times 9 she began at stone 6 and joined the 5 to the 4, answer 54.

Easy isn't it?

See if you can finish your nine times table this way.

"There's no need for an answer, is there?" asked Smiler.

Magico's Magic Square

93 Magico says: "Bet you can't put the numbers 3, 4, 6, 7, 8, 9 in the square here so that the rows of numbers across, down, and along each diagonal each add up to 15, the magic number of the square!"

Where in the World?

94 What was the biggest volcano?

95 What is the longest bridge in the world?

96 What was the biggest earthquake on record?

97 What is the wettest place in the world?

98 What is the longest river in the world?

99 What is the San Andreas fault?

100 What is the highest mountain in the world?

101 What is the coldest place in the world?

102 What is the hottest place in the world?

103 What is the largest lake in the world?

104 Name the three great oceans.

105 Which sea is so salty you can't sink in it?

106 Which is the biggest continent?

107 Where is the smallest island with a name?

108 Where is the Grand Canyon?

109 Two animals are shown on Australia's coat of arms. What are they?

110 What country is an entire continent?

111 What are the horse latitudes?

112 Is the Tropic of Capricorn north or south of the Equator? And the Tropic of Cancer?

113 Which is the biggest sheep-raising country in the world?

114 What is a deciduous tree?

115 Where is the Sahara desert?

116 Where is the Gobi desert?

117 What is a book of maps called?

118 Why did Christopher Columbus call the islands off North America, the West Indies?

Magico's Magic Line

119 Magico has drawn a whiter-than-white line with just six black blobs he marked on paper. What's so magical about it? Well, cover up five of the blobs and the line disappears *just like that*! It's another of the optical illusions so dear to Magico's heart.

Magico's Number Trick

120 Here is Magico's favourite number trick. It's so simple you can try it on your unsuspecting friends. Just practise it a bit before you do though.

It's best done with a lot of people: the more there are, the more mysterious it seems.

This is what you say to your audience:

"I want you all to think of a number between 6 and 10, inclusive. That means you can choose 6, 7, 8, 9 or 10. "Now I'm going to choose a number of my own" – here you write the number 4 on a slip of paper and put it in an envelope – "and I'll give it to one of you for safe-keeping." You hand the sealed envelope to a member of your audience. Remember, your audience does not know the number you wrote down.

You continue:

"Now I'm going to ask each one of you to do a little sum. I want you to add 5 to the number you thought of. You should now have a two-figure number in the teens. Cross off the first figure, a one, and add it to the other 'ones' figure. Take the answer away from the number you first thought of and . . . the answer is in the envelope. You should all have the same number!"

If they have followed your instructions correctly, they will all have the number four in the envelope.

Here is an example to show you how the trick goes.

You put "4" in the envelope. A friend thinks of 7, say.

You say: "Add 5."

He adds 5 to 7 to get 12. He crosses off the 1 and puts it under the 2:

$$
\begin{array}{r}
1\;2 \\
+\;\;1 \\
\hline
3
\end{array}
$$

to get 3:

He takes 3 from his "thought" number, 7 and gets 4 – which is the number in the envelope. See the answer for how the trick works.

Creepy-Crawlies

121 From how far away can one moth scent another?

122 Ants keep "cows" for their "milk". Do you know what insect their "cows" are?

123 Which insect lives seventeen years underground?

124 What is the dance of the bees?

125 Bees tell other bees where to find flowers with nectar, which they make into honey. How do they do it?

126 How do bees in a hive keep warm in winter?

127 Where are a grasshopper's ears?

128 How many legs has a centipede?
How many has a millipede?

129 What is the fastest flying insect?

130 What is a katydid?

131 What is a silkworm – a butterfly, a moth, or a worm?

132 How does a silkworm make silk?

133 What are a silkworm's front feet for?

134 Why does a silkworm make silk?

135 What does a silkworm do inside its cocoon?

136 **The Heavy Hippo Puzzle**

A heavy happy hippo weighs 1 tonne plus half his own weight. Now tell me, how much does the hippo weigh?

Serena's Screechy Viola

137 When Serena played her viola it made such a screechy noise, poor Smiler just sat and howled. You see, she could not get it to sing sweetly. What was the cure? She asked Magico to help her. He told her it was all a matter of numbers and wrote down the words NEVER SINGS and the number 0 to 9 beneath them, like this:

N E V E R   S I N G S
0 1 2 3 4   5 6 7 8 9

He then told her to do the following. (You do the same for yourself and see if you don't get the same answer – but choose your *own* numbers.)

Magico said:

"Choose two numbers from SINGS and one from NEVER and write them down as a three-figure number. But you must make sure that the first and last figures are at least two apart. So 584 wouldn't do because 5 and 4 are only one apart."

Serena chose 6 and 8 from SINGS and 3 from NEVER, and wrote down: 683. Magico went on: "Now reverse the number."

Serena wrote 386.

"Take the smaller from the bigger," Magico instructed her.

Serena did her sum:

$$\begin{array}{r} 683 \\ -386 \\ \hline 297 \end{array}$$

Now turn the answer round and write it underneath and add:

$$\begin{array}{r} 297 \\ +792 \\ \hline 1089 \end{array}$$

"Abracadabra!" exclaimed Magico. "You want to play *forte*, don't you Serena? So multiply by 40."

Serena did so:

$$\begin{array}{r} 1089 \\ \times\ 40 \\ \hline \end{array}$$

Well, you can do this for her, can't you? Turn the answer back into letters and you will see what she needed to put on the bow of her viola to make it sing sweetly and loudly (*forte*).

Try Magico's recipe with your own numbers and – abracadabra – it will always give the same answer. How's that for number magic!

The Sky at Night

138 Can you name the nine planets, and give their order from the sun?

139 One of the planets' "day" is longer than its "year". Which planet is it?

140 What is the evening star? Clue: It is also called the morning star and yet it isn't a star!

141 What is a white dwarf?

142 What is the Milky Way?

143 Which is the nearest galaxy?

144 Can you name these constellations of stars? Choose from these names: Cassiopeia, Orion's Belt, The Plough, The Little Bear.

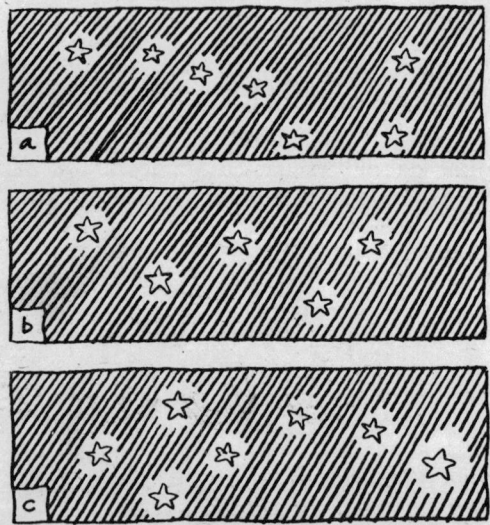

145 How hot is the Sun? How much hotter do you think it is than a lighted cigarette?

146 What is a light year — a period of time or a distance?

147 Which is the nearest star — after the Sun?

Serena's Silly Slip

148 Serena had just typed three letters to three friends inviting them to come to tea. She addressed the three envelopes, correctly, for once! Being a dizzy girl, she popped the letters, one in each envelope without looking at them, and sealed them up. Smiler had noticed that two of the letters did go in their correct envelopes. What is the chance that only two letters went in the right envelopes, and only two? (This is a catch question!)

A Triangle of Coins

149 Serena laid out ten coins in the form of a triangle, pointing upwards like this:

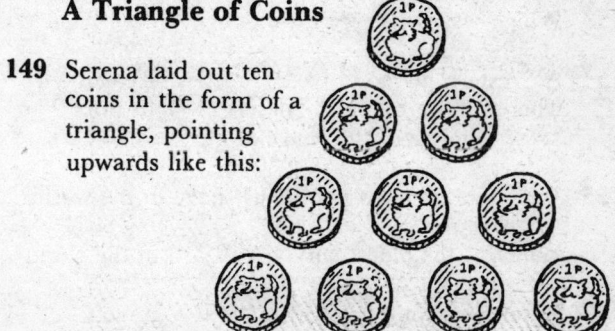

She says: "Can you make the triangle point downwards by moving only three coins?"

Smiler's Miler-Walkies

150 Smiler likes to go for a good long walk every morning, noon, and evening. A good mile (2 km) three times a day. He calls them his "milers". Serena wrote this little multiplication sum:

$$\begin{array}{r} \text{S M I L E R} \\ \times\ 3 \\ \hline \text{M I L E R S} \end{array}$$

Each letter stands for a number, the same number wherever it appears. Can you find the numbers that fit this sum? Smiler's hint: R stands for 4.

Dinosaurs and Snakes alive!

151 What does *dinosaur* mean?

152 Which was the biggest dinosaur?

153 Which was the fiercest dinosaur?

154 A Western diamond-backed rattlesnake can tell where a rabbit is in the desert at night from 2 km away. How does the snake do it?

155 Which is the most poisonous snake in the world?

156 Which is the oldest surviving lizard in the world?

157 What is a Komodo Dragon? Is it a dragon?

158 Which frog barks like a dog? English Common Frog, Tree Climbing Frog, South American Bullfrog.

159 Is a slowworm a snake, a worm or a lizard?
Clue: It has no legs.

160 Magico's Box Trick

How many balls are in the box now?
Just count the balls in each picture.

Magico's Magic Whiteboard

161 Magico has set up a whiteboard on an easel for his next trick. You can see it plainly, can't you? It's white on white, only the board is whiter than white. Yet cover up the black corners and what happens? Why, the whiteness seems to fade. The board was just an illusion, *of course!*

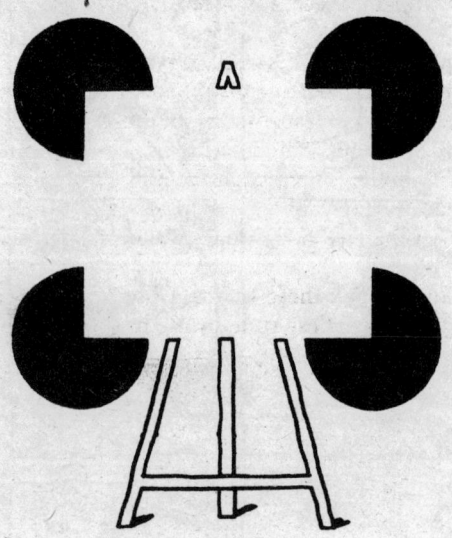

The Chiming Clock Puzzle

162 Serena's old grandfather clock has gone wrong, yet again! It chimes three times at one o'clock, four times at two o'clock, and so on.

To make matters worse it is half-an-hour fast. What is the correct time when her clock has just chimed seven?

All about Us

163 How did people wash themselves before soap was invented?

164 How was soap probably invented?

165 How did they make the colours for their clothes in the time of Queen Elizabeth I? What did they use, for instance, for green, yellow, red and blue?

166 There have been some very unusual styles of hairdressing worn by women through ages, but nothing so extraordinary as those worn by the ladies of the French Court at the time of Marie Antoinette. The foolish looking ship on the lady's head towered above her head. How far do you think the top of the mast was from her chin?

167 Can you put these hairdressing styles in order from the earliest style to the more recent?

168 How fast do our finger nails grow?

169 How fast does our hair grow?

170 What is astigmatism?

171 How do we get silk cloth?

The Hippos and Rhinos Puzzle

172 Magico was on safari when he spotted a herd of
hippos and a set of rhinos grazing happily
together. He took this snap of them. Some of
them were grey and some were white. See if you
can sort them out into sets by drawing rings
round them. Draw a ring right round all the
hippos. How many are there? Now draw another
ring round all the grey animals. How many are
there of them? Finally, how many animals are
either a hippo or grey-coloured? Hint: Count the
animals inside the two rings you've drawn.

Smiler's Sums

173 Smiler has been doing his sums. But as usual he's got most of them wrong. Can you correct them for him?

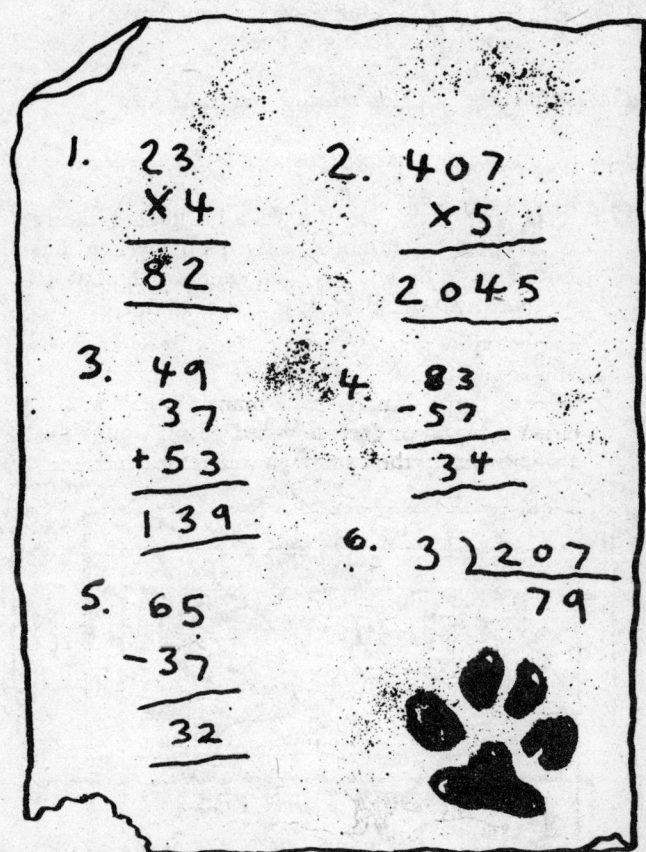

1. $\begin{array}{r} 23 \\ \times 4 \\ \hline 82 \end{array}$

2. $\begin{array}{r} 407 \\ \times 5 \\ \hline 2045 \end{array}$

3. $\begin{array}{r} 49 \\ 37 \\ +53 \\ \hline 139 \end{array}$

4. $\begin{array}{r} 83 \\ -57 \\ \hline 34 \end{array}$

5. $\begin{array}{r} 65 \\ -37 \\ \hline 32 \end{array}$

6. $3\overline{)207}$ 79

Wild Animals

174 How can you tell the difference between an Indian and an African elephant? Tell at a glance, I mean.

175 Where does the rhinoceros with one horn, and the rhino with two horns live?

176 What does an elephant use his tusks for?

177 What do apes use grass stalks for?

178 This is a hyrax. Yes, it looks a bit like a mixture of a rabbit and a mouse, only it's bigger and has hornier feet. Serena bets you cannot tell what animal it is related to. It is one of these:

SMILER'S ONCERS

Smiler: "How many hippos can you get into an empty mini?"
Answer: None – because it's empty.

SMILER'S ONCERS

Smiler says: "Have you heard the
one about the two Irishmen who
managed to save themselves from a
sinking ship by rowing away
in a row boat? When they got
to a desert island they broke up the boat
to make a raft. . . "

179 What animal is the panda's nearest relative?

180 What is a mud-puppy – a young dog, a mudlark, or a salamander?

181 What animal has a beak like a duck, fur and webbed feet like an otter, a poison spur in its hind leg like a snake, a tail like a beaver, and a shoulder bone like a crocodile? It also lays eggs like a hen.

182 Why do bats squeak when they fly by night?

183 When ostriches hatch out of their eggs, they do something very unusual: it's called *crêching* (say it KRAY-SHING). What is crêching?

184 What is the tallest animal?

185 What is the fastest running animal?

186 What is a dugong?

187 Which animal lays the most eggs – a sturgeon, an oyster, or a common toad?

188 Which animal lives to the greatest age?

189 How can you tell the difference between a Bactrian camel and a dromedary?

190 What is the odd one out? It does not belong as all the others do to the same family.

elephant	opossum
eagle	dog
cat	

191 Here are the footprints of ten animals. Can you say which footprint belongs to which animal? The animals are: hedgehog, badger, red deer, horse, rat, rabbit, hare, fox, wolf, otter.

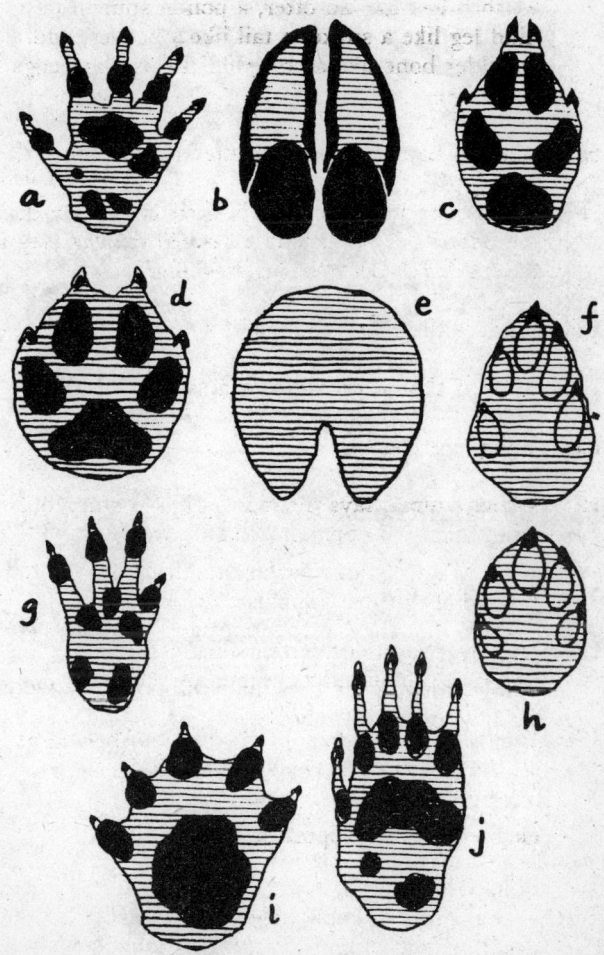

Snow-blind?

192 Can you spot a dog in this snowy scene? What dog is it? Hint: *101 D. . . . . .* a book and a film.

193 The Safari Puzzler

When Magico was on safari in Africa, he sighted a group of thirteen animals. A closer look revealed that they were hippos and ostriches. He counted forty-six legs in all.

Now can you say how many hippos there were and how many ostriches?

Science Surprises!

194 Eggs-actly!

Serena wants to know how to tell whether an egg is bad or not, without cracking it. How can she do this?

Electric Mystery Cards

195 Here are some electric mystery cards that Magico has devised for you. Each card has three metal buttons A, B and C along one side, and three more X, Y and Z along the opposite side. Magico has written a chart to show how the buttons are to be wired up. What you've got to do is to draw the wires on the card from Magico's chart. The first one is drawn to show how you do it.

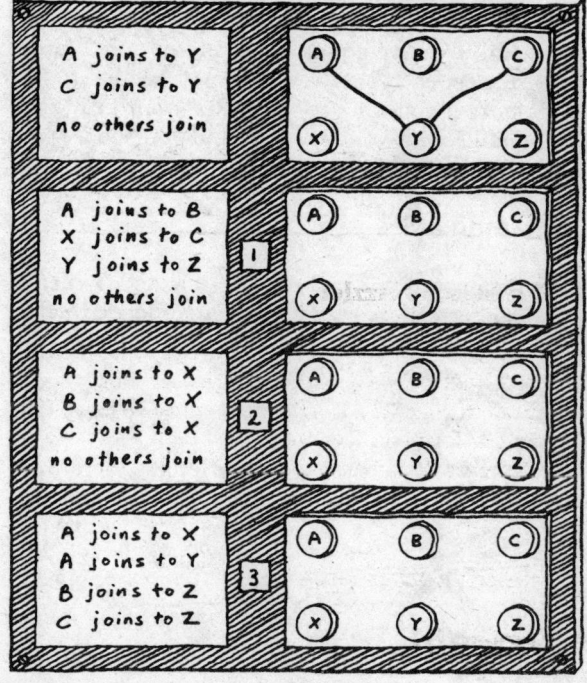

A joins to Y
C joins to Y
no others join

A joins to B
X joins to C
Y joins to Z
no others join

1

A joins to X
B joins to X
C joins to X
no others join

2

A joins to X
A joins to Y
B joins to Z
C joins to Z

3

196 Does a cup of water weigh more or less if you float a cork in it?

The Rolling Tins Race

197 Magico was at his stall at the Fun Fair. He had a sloping plank and two tins, one a large one, the other small. He was offering bets to anyone who put his money down:
"Which tin will win, rolling down the slope?"
Well, which tin do *you* think will win? The answer is a surprising fact of science.

Make your Watch Tick Louder

198 Here's a trick you can try. Take off your wrist watch, if you've got one, and place it on a large bare wooden table. Now you may be able to hear its ticks if you are very still. Rest your head on the table with your ear to it and you should hear the ticking much more clearly.

Two on a See-saw

199 Serena sat at one end of a see-saw and Smiler at the other end, with a picnic basket loaded with goodies and weighing 20 kilos.

Smiler weighs 10 kilos less than the picnic basket.
Can you say how much Serena weighs?

Black-and-White Jumble

200 I bet you can't make head or tail of this jumble. But turn this book upside down and stare hard and I think you may make something of it. What can you see?

Tall Tales and Books

201 How many plays did William Shakespeare write?

202 Who wrote *The Canterbury Tales*?

203 What was the first book printed by moveable type?

204 Who was William Caxton?

205 Who was Wynkin de Worde?
His surname is a clue.
Extra clue: Look at the last quiz.

Magico's Lens

206 Magico slips a circular glass lens out of his
waistcoat pocket and holds it up for all to see. It
is perfectly round, is it not? Now he holds it in
front of the pattern of spokes you see before you
and. . . lo and behold it is no longer round. Or is
it? Just check by tracing over it, just to make
sure it is not yet another of the magician's
illusions.

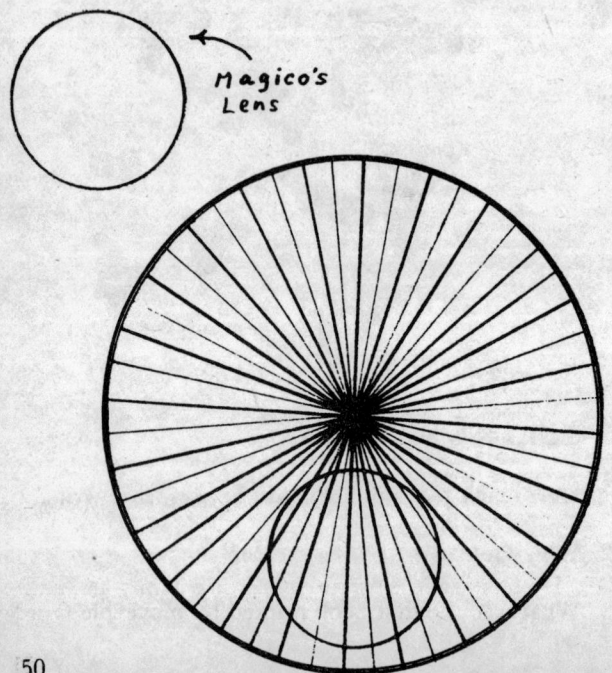

Magico's
Lens

207 Who was Baron Munchausen?

208 What are the *Arabian Nights*?

209 Who was Scheherazade?

Smiler's Collar and Lead Puzzle

210 Serena bought Smiler a new collar and lead for his birthday. They cost £3 together. But the collar cost £1 more than the lead.
How much did the lead cost?

211 Moses sent ten plagues upon Pharaoh and the people of Egypt. Can you name three of them?

Who made it First?

212 Who invented the telescope?

213 Who invented the telephone?

214 Who invented the radio?

215 These are all names of inventors. What invention did they all help create?
Joseph Cugnot, Karl Benz, Gottlieb Daimler, Louis Renault.

216 When was the first powered aeroplane flight, and who made it?

217 Who invented the bicycle with pneumatic (inflatable) tyres?

218 How big was the front wheel of a penny-farthing bicycle?

219 All these names were given to one machine at one time or another. Do you know what it is? Bone-shaker, ordinary, célérifère, vélocifere, hobby-horse, dandy-horse, draisenne.

220 Who invented, but never built, the submarine?

221 Who invented the Bunsen burner?

222 Who invented the railway engine? James Watt, Richard Trevithick, George Stephenson.

223 What is margarine, and who invented it?

Magico's Sleight of Hand

224 What is this that Magico holds in his hand? Why, it's clearly a three-pronged tuning fork. Funny, you think, tuning forks only have two prongs, not three. Look on the opposite page and you see all's well: the fork has only two prongs. . . yet somehow it's the same fork. "Now, that's what I call a real illusion. . . if an illusion can be real," declares Magico.

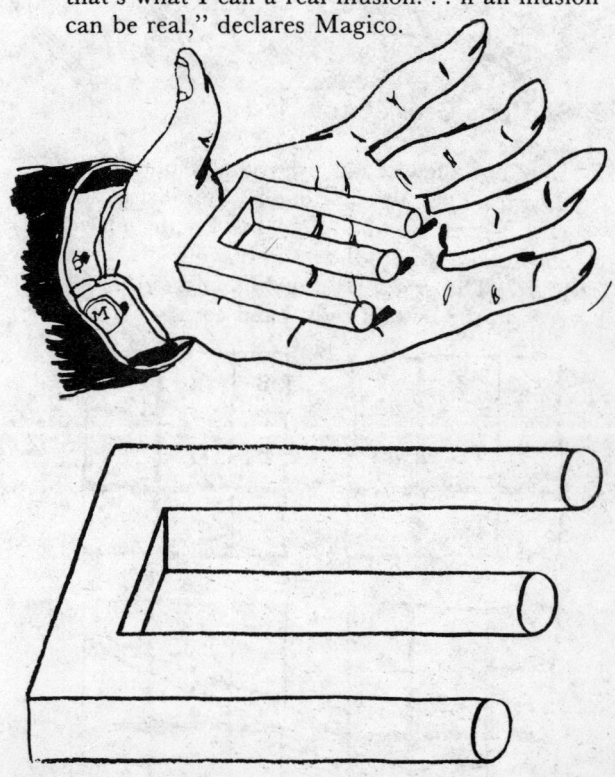

Smiler's Cross-Sums

225 Here are a few of the cross-sums Smiler likes to do. He's done the first one for you just to show how it goes. You add across to get the answers shown of 5 and 9, then add downwards to get 7 and 7. The grand total of 5+9 and also of 7+7 goes in the bottom right hand corner: 14.

5	9	
4	10	

8	7	
9	11	

13	5	
10	12	

11	12	
13	14	

Magico's Lines

226 Magico has two rods, apparently floating in the air at the foot of his easel. Of course, the top line is longer than the lower one. You'd better make sure this is not another of Magico's illusions.

Serena's Strawberry Flan

227 Serena had made a flan and in her usual way was trying to puzzle out how to cut it up into the greatest number of pieces with just four straight cuts. Can you draw the lines on this flan? Smiler made nine pieces. But I know you can do better, can't you?

Test your Word Power

Potty Proverbs

228 Smiler has been doggedly learning some well-known sayings and proverbs from Serena. But, as usual, he has got them mixed up. Can you unscramble them for him by writing the *correct* word in the space? It's pretty obvious why he got some of them wrong!

1 A miss is as good as a *smile!* (. . . . . . .)
2 A rolling stone gathers no *bread*. (. . . . . . .)
3 Don't *bark* (. . . . . . .) over spilt milk.
4 Charity begins at *once*. (. . . . . . .)
5 Discretion is the better part of *value* (. . . . .)
6 Don't count your *bones* (. . . . .) before they are *dug up* (. . . . .)
7 Out of the frying pan, into the *kennel*. (. . . . .)
8 The early bird catches the *bone*. (. . . . . . .)
9 When the cat's away the *dogs* (. . . . .) will play.
10 Sauce for the goose is sauce for the *panda*. (. . . . .)
11 Out of sight, out of *the wind* (. . . . .)

SMILER'S ONCERS

Smiler: "How many months have thirty days?"
Answer: All but February – or 11 months.

Laddergram Puzzle

229 Serena likes playing with words.
One of her favourite word puzzles
is to change one word into another.
You change one letter at a time,
and every time you change a letter
you must make a new word. Here is
how Serena changed BACK into LINE:

B	A	N	K
B	A	N	E
L	A	N	E
L	I	N	E

See if you can change these words;
Serena has given you some clues.

evening
an elephant
has two
a job of work

D	U	S	T
T	A	N	K

the only one
miss
not found

L	A	N	E
P	O	S	T

outside of tree
not light
for throwing

B	A	S	K
D	I	R	T

headpiece
tail shake
direction
speak

P	I	G
S	T	Y

Poetry Puzzles

230 Serena has written out some verses from well-known poems, which she is sure Smiler (and you) will know.
What he (and you) have to do is to fill in the missing words, which Serena has given at the side of the poem.

Jabberwocky by Lewis Carroll

'Twas brillig, and the slithy.	mimsy
Did gyre and gimble in the . . . . :	outgrabe
All . . . .were the borrogroves,	wabe
And the mome raths	toves

The Pied Piper of Hamelin by Robert Browning

(The rats) they fought the dogs, and	soup
killed the . . . . ,	cats
and bit the . . . . . . in the cradles,	vats
And ate the cheeses out of the . . . . . .,	babies
And licked the . . . . from the cook's	ladles
own	

The Owl and the Pussycat by Edward Lear

They sailed away for a year and a . . .,	
To the land where the Bong-. . .,	Piggy-wig
grows;	nose
And there in a wood a P. . . . .-. . . stood,	day
With a ring at the end of its	tree

58

To-and-fro words

231   "Pay attention, Smiler!" said Serena a little sharply.

"We're going to learn some special words." Smiler cocked one ear.

"Some words," went on Serena, "spell the same forwards as backwards. Like noon. See if you can work out what they are from these clues."

pieces of music for one
    performer
mother
orange seed
flat
feat of daring
his face went. . . .
than a beetroot

Fill the grid in correctly and the arrowed column spells the name of whomever it is Serena is talking to.

Male and Female Words

232 Can you give the feminine form of these masculine words? The ones marked with an asterisk (*) are hard. If you know *them*, you are doing very well. The answer to the first is *actress*.

actor. . . . .
author. . . . .
duke. . . . .
emperor. . . . . . .
heir. . . . .
host. . . . .
manager. . . . .
god. . . . .
tiger. . . . .
*marquis. . . . .
*earl. . . . . . .
*lad. . . . . . .
*wizard. . . . .

SMILER'S ONCERS

Smiler: "What word is always pronounced incorrectly?"
Answer: Incorrectly.

ANSWERS

1

WHITE	BLACK	WHITE	BLACK
with chimney	with chimney	without chimney	without chimney
2	2	3	3

2 All sea animals speak. Seals in the icy cold Arctic call to each other with a loud, sad cry. They are very noisy about it. Killer whales speak by whistling and making cries.

3 Humpback whales are called singing whales. They sing, roar, and bellow and mew like a seagull. Their singing sounds like the clanking of chains and the squeaking of doors.

4 This is their way of finding their way about, when the sea is cloudy or at night when they cannot see underwater. They can see very well in clear water. They use their ears to pick up the echo of their "clicks", just as bats use the echo of their squeaks. They make thousands of "clicks" in a second. But they don't have a voice box as you or I do. When they "click" they do not make bubbles in the water. These "clicks" are too high for you or me to hear. We need a special electrical receiver to hear them.

5 Yes, they do. But this is not the same as their "clicks". They blow bubbles through the blow-holes on the top of their heads. When a dolphin blows one large bubble, it is a warning to another dolphin of danger. The Ancient Greeks knew that dolphins spoke to one another.

6 They also whistle to speak to one another. We do not know how they whistle for, as I have said before, they have no voice-box. The whistles come out of the blow-holes on top of their heads.

7 Dolphins kept in tanks have about 2,000 "words". These are different whistles and "boops". One dolphin will use these words to tell another dolphin what he has seen, or to tell him of danger, or to cry "help". A dolphin who has been in a tank a long time will tell a newcomer what the tank is like by his whistles.

8 It is a strange, sad, moving noise. They make these noises underwater. Dolphins can be trained to sing in the open air. But they have to be kept in a large tank and taught to do this. They learn to sing quite easily.

9 The only route that takes in an even number of stations is ABCDEFIGH and Funville, making ten stations in all. All the other routes give an odd number of stations.

10 A hand is just over 10 cm – roughly the width of a man's palm.

11 Eohippus was about the size of a small terrier dog. It stood about 60 cm (at the shoulder).

12 Ten hands, or 102 cm.

13 Dale, Shetland, Dartmoor, Welsh Mountain, Highland, Fell, Connemara, Exmoor, New Forest. The others are names of breeds of horses.

14 Horses used to run wild over grasslands full of flies, so over the years they developed the skin "flick" to get rid of them. (Horses cannot scratch themselves with their feet as a dog can, though they can scratch their bellies in a half-hearted sort of way!)

15 A horse has four feet with hooves. Each foot is really like our five fingers grown into one; the hoof is like our nails. A horse uses its four hooves for kicking and running. The hoof grows like finger nails, and the blacksmith has to pare (cut) it back every so often.

16 The frog is the triangle of tough flesh underneath each hoof. The flesh is called *cartilage*. It is rather like hardened gristle. It is full of blood.

underside of horse's hoof

the frog

17 As the horse has very long legs for its body, the heart needs a little help to pump all the blood back up again. The frog under the horse's hoof is to pump blood back up the horse's legs. Each time the horse steps on the ground, the frog gets squashed. This forces the blood in it back up the leg. So the frogs under each hoof are really four extra "hearts" helping to pump the blood around the body.

18 It is possible to tell a horse's age by looking at its teeth. A horse has milk teeth like young children. These all drop out by the time the horse is four-and-a-half years old. By five years, it has all its adult teeth. At ten years a special groove appears in some of the teeth. A vet looks at all these signs to tell a horse's age.

19 Cornelia could hardly have let her know if she hadn't received a postcard!

20 Put three matches on the table to make a triangle. Stand the other three matches up in a tent at the corners of the first triangle. You have a tetrahedron.

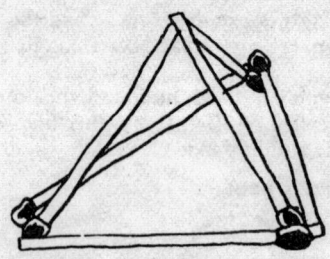

21 She was Queen of a tribe of Britons at the time the Romans conquered Britain. She fought the Romans in AD 61.

22 Queen Victoria. She reigned for sixty-four years; she came to the throne in 1837 and died in 1901.

23 Benjamin Disraeli.

24 The shooting started off the First World War, the most terrible war the world has ever known. Sarajevo is in Yugoslavia.

25 Christopher Columbus in 1492.

26 Spanish explorers brought the potato back to Europe from Peru, Bolivia, and Colombia, in South America, in 1550.

27 It took place in October 1854 in the Battle of Balaclava during the Crimean War which was fought between Russia and the Allies – Britain, France, Sardinia and Turkey. The Charge of the Light Brigade was the suicidal charge of 600 British cavalry against the Russians in the Battle of Balaclava, which the Allies won.

28 Leonardo da Vinci, who lived in Italy from 1452 to 1519. It is one of the most famous paintings in the world; it is also known as *La Gioconda*. Leonardo painted it in 1503.

29 It was the name once given to China. Marco Polo travelled to Cathay.

30 It was the year 46 BC when Julius Caesar was Emperor of the Roman Empire. The Romans found that their calendar was three months ahead of the schedule fixed by the seasons; so the calendar showed March when it was still mid-winter. To put it right, Julius Caesar ruled that the year 46 BC should have 445 days and so began the *Julian calendar* with the standard 365 days a year.

31 The Julian calendar year was about eleven minutes fourteen seconds longer than the Sun's year. By 1752, Britain was eleven days out from the Sun's year, so George II ordered Britain to change to a new calendar, the Gregorian calendar. But when he did so the people "lost" the days between September 2 and September 14. They really believed they had lost those days and they gathered in the streets of London to protest, shouting "Give us back our eleven days!"

32 King Edward VI (1547–1553) came to the throne when he was only ten. King Edward VIII came to the throne on January 20, 1936, and abdicated less than a year later.

33 Henry's six wives were:
      Catherine of Aragon, divorced.
      Anne Boleyn, beheaded.
      Jane Seymour, died soon after the birth of her son, later Edward VI.
      Anne of Cleves, divorced.
      Catherine Howard, beheaded.
      Catherine Parr, survived Henry.

34 Sir Francis Drake. He was playing bowls on Plymouth Hoe on June 31, 1588, when the Spanish Armada was sighted sailing into the English Channel. His fellow commanders wanted to put to sea at once but, the story goes, Drake made his famous remark, won the game, and beat the Spaniards too!

35 Her statement "If I'm not innocent, my name's not Serena Dippity!" means in logic "If I'm Serena Dippity, I'm innocent." Well, since you know she *is* Serena Dippity, then she must be innocent. That's logic.

36

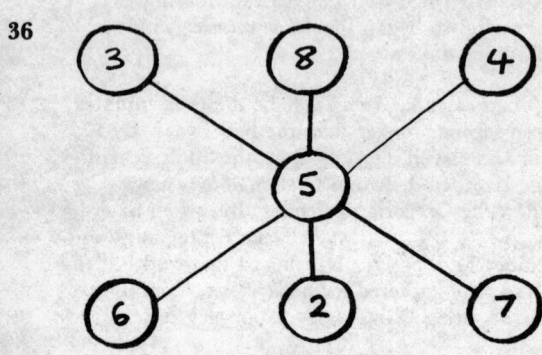

37 Four socks. They might all match or the first three she chose might all be different colours so that the fourth would have to match one of them.

38 It is the name for beads, black, purple or white, made from shells. Indians from the east of North America once used wampum as money. The Indians gave William Penn, the founder of Pennsylvania, a wampum belt as a token of their respect for him.

39 Maundy money is the silver coins, originally English shillings, now 10p coins, given to the poor by the King or Queen on Maundy Thursday. Maundy Thursday comes three days before Easter. The word *Maundy* comes from the Latin *mandatum* meaning a commandment.

40 Blood money, or bot money was money paid, during the Middle Ages, by a murderer to the relatives of his victim. The price was according to the kind of murder and the importance of the victim. You read in history books of "bootless crimes", which is another form of "botless crimes" – that is a murder in which the murderer has not paid the relatives blood money. Nowadays bribes paid for informing on a criminal are called "blood money".

41 In Italy, where small coins are worth very little, sweets are often given as small change in some shops.

42 In North America in 1619 and afterwards. In the states of Virginia, Maryland and North Carolina tobacco was used as money; it was worth three *shillings* a pound weight – that's about six shillings in their currency then for a kilo of tobacco. In those days to pay a bill of £225 you would need to be able to carry a roll of tobacco weighing 70 kilos under your arm! That's the weight of a sack of wheat. So you can see why paper money and coins came into use.

43 Spear-shaped bronze coins, the earliest money, were used in China about 4000 years ago.

44 The Ancient Greeks minted the first silver coins in 600 BC.

45 The Chinese, who invented paper, used paper money as early as the 1300s.

46 Silver and gold coins were once worth the face value stamped on them for they had that worth of silver or gold in them. People used to "clip" bits off the edge of the coins and sell it as silver or gold. So to stop the clipping of coins, the edges of coins were *milled*.

47 First she weighed eggs *a* and *b* against *c* and *d*. Suppose *c* and *d* went down. That meant *a* or *b* was the lighter egg. Then she weighed *a* against *b*. If *c* and *d* went up, then *c* or *d* was the lighter egg. Then she weighed *c* against *d*. Whichever egg went up was the lighter egg. So she did it in two weighings.

48 Pick up the coin at the foot of the cross and place it on the middle coin.

49 Only one hour. Serena had forgotten that the alarm would go off at nine o'clock that very evening!

50 Her black cat.

51 The witch of Endor is in the Bible, in the first book of Samuel, chapter 28, verse 7. She lived in the town of Endor, in Palestine, and now called Indur. Saul, the first king of the Hebrews, went in disguise to see the witch before the battle with the Philistines. He asked her to summon up the ghost of the prophet Samuel. At first she was afraid to do so because Saul had banished all the wizards and witches – all who had familiar spirits – from Israel. Finally she was persuaded to raise the ghost of Samuel who prophesied Saul's death on the morrow.

52 A wizard or a male witch.

53 The Loch Ness Monster is a monster that looks like a brontosaurus that is supposed to live in the famous loch of that name in Scotland. A monk in the 1200s is the first to have reported seeing it. But the monster, nick-named "Nessy", has been "sighted" several times in the last fifty years; Nessy has even been photographed. Submarines have searched the dark depths of the lake but no such creature has actually been found.

54 He is one of America's best-loved folklore characters. He appears in a story by Washington Irving. He is a cheerful ne'er-do-well who prefers hunting and fishing to farming and listening to his wife's nagging. He falls asleep for twenty years. When he wakes up, he finds his wife is dead and that everything in his village is changed, but his children recognize him and the villagers finally welcome him back.

55 He was the wizard in the story *The Wizard of Oz* written by Frank Baum.

56 It was a mythical creature, half man and half horse. It had the head, arms and trunk of a man, and the body and four legs and tail of a horse.

57 They were twin heroes in the Greek myths. They were the sons of Zeus, also called Jupiter. They had power over the winds and the waves and in the myth, they were placed together in the night sky in the constellation *Gemini*, the Twins.

58 They were the legendary founders of Rome. They were the twin sons of Mars, god of war. They were thrown into the Tiber in a basket and rescued and cared for by a she-wolf. Romulus one day killed Remus in a quarrel and then founded the city of Rome on the banks of the Tiber.

59 The Greek Goddess Medusa, one of the three Gorgons. She also had a *petrifying* stare; to *petrify* means *to turn to stone*. The Gorgons were so ugly that anyone who looked on them was turned to stone.

60 Perseus killed her. He looked at her in the mirror of his shiny shield and so could cut off her head with his sword. If he had looked her in the eye, he would have been turned to stone.

61 Three hours – not, as you might guess, four hours.

62 4 divided by a ½ is 8 because there are 8 halves in 4 wholes. Add 2 and the answer is 4 + 2 = 6.

63 You'll never believe this, but it is a plant and it eats flies, alive! It grows in the south-eastern United States. It has spiky leaves which snap shut to trap unwary flies and other little insects. It is a meat-eater. It grows in bogs and marshes.

64 The Gingko tree belongs to a group of trees that lived millions of years ago. It grows wild in China but is kept in gardens in Britain and North America. It is also called the maidenhair tree.

65 The tallest and biggest tree is the redwood tree, or sequoia. The tallest redwood tree stands 111.8 metres. The biggest has a girth of twenty-four metres.

66 The French aviator Louis Blériot in a monoplane on July 25, 1909.

67 Amy Johnson. She made the trip in nineteen-and-a-half days in 1930.

68 He was a dwarf just over a metre tall. His real name was Charles Stratton and he was exhibited as a freak in Barnum and Bailey's circus.

69 The *Cullinan* diamond, found in 1905 in the Premier mine in the South African diamond fields. It weighed about 680 grams.

70 T-tropics, F-fresh water, S-summer, W-winter, WNA-winter North Atlantic; LR means the ship is registered with Lloyd's insurance company. They are loading markings painted on the side of a ship's hull. They show how much cargo the ship can safely carry in different waters of the world. A ship loaded "down to the Plimsoll line" is loaded to its full capacity. The Plimsoll line was invented by a British merchant, Samuel Plimsoll, to prevent the overloading of ships at a time when this was a common practice.

71 It is a channel, tunnel or pipeline for carrying water from one place to another. The Roman aqueducts are the most famous ever built.

72 It is a stringed instrument like a lute, played in Rumania. It has four pairs of strings; the player plays it with a plectrum, a short length of quill.

73 **a** harpsichord **b** virginal **c** spinet **d** clavichord **e** piano

74 For adding up; the Chinese and the Japanese still use them in shops.

75 The purple came from the dye of the cuttle fish.

76 Shields in heraldry. This is what they look like:

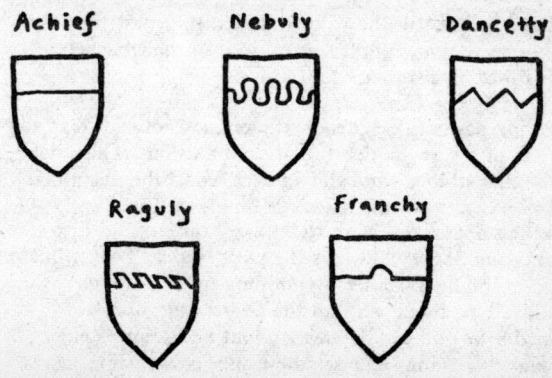

Achief Nebuly Dancetty

Raguly Franchy

77 You look at its scales under a magnifying glass or a microscope. Then you count the rings on a scale. Each ring means the fish has lived one year. For fish's scales are like rings you can see on the end of a log cut from a tree.

78 Persian carpets. The signs are traditional ones.

79 She must put a metal skewer through each of them. The metal conducts heat well and takes it to the centre of the potato thus cooking it much more quickly.

80 The brim is actually bigger.

81 Well, you should have one complete ring, with a loop in it. Pull the loop tight, but do so carefully. And you should have a knot in the strip! Press it down firmly and you'll find the knot is in the shape of a five-sided shape, a pentagon, like this:

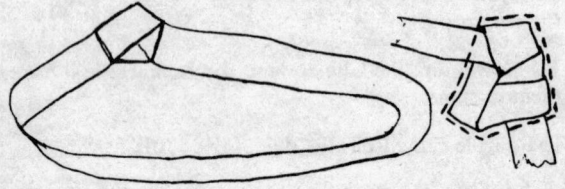

82 Dogs did this in the wild to flatten the grass to make their bed. They don't *need* to do it in their baskets. Instinct makes them do it.

83 A dog pants to keep cool. Its tongue cools down in the rush of air as the dog breathes in and out. This cools the dog's blood, and this in turn, cools the dog's body.

84 When dogs lived in the wild, they ran around in packs, and one dog was always the pack leader. They would greet the pack leader by jumping up and wagging their tails. This made sure all the dogs would obey the leader in times of danger without hesitation. Really your dog thinks you are the leader of his pack.

85 Dogs can hear higher-pitched sounds than we can. These high-pitched sounds are called *ultra-sonic* sounds. We cannot hear a dog whistle because the sound is too high for our ears to hear.

86 Men can talk to sheepdogs by whistles. One whistle means "go left", another "go right", and another "stop", and so on. Some islanders in the Mediterranean Sea also talk to each other by whistle!

87 Cats do this to exercise their claws. A cat's claws go in and out of a sheath, and must be kept strong. Wild cats need claws like this so that they can catch their prey. Domestic cats are simply practising what they need to do in the wild on the curtains and furniture.

88 Cats can't really see in the dark. But they can see quite well in dim light. A cat's eye has a dark slit for the pupil which lets light into the eye. In bright light the slit is narrow and lets in little light. In dim light the slit grows round and lets in lots more light.

89 All but the lion, puma, civet, lynx, ocelot and tiger are domestic cats.

90 They are all domestic breeds of dogs.

91 Smiler's x must go in the bottom right hand corner.

94 Krakatoa between the islands of Sumatra and Java erupted in 1883 with the greatest explosion known. It killed 36,000 people and threw out 20 cubic kilometres of lava and other solids.

95 The Pontchartrain Causeway Bridge in North America with a total length of just over thirty-eight kilometres.

96 The Lisbon earthquake of October 31, 1755.

97 Cherrapunji in Assam where 2644 cm of rain fell between August 1860 and July 1861.

98 The River Nile which is 6656 km long.

99 It is a 320-kilometre (200-mile) crack or fault running the length of California in North America.

100 Mount Everest, at 8848 metres or nearly nine kilometres.

101 Vostok in the Antarctic where, in 1960, a temperature of −88.3°C was recorded.

102 Azizia, Libya, where a temperature of 58.0°C was recorded in 1922. San Luis in Mexico has also had as high a temperature.

103 Lake Superior is the largest body of fresh water in the world. It covers 81,459 square kilometres. The Caspian Sea is larger but it is called a sea.

104 The Pacific, Atlantic and Indian oceans.

105 The Dead Sea, on the border between Israel and Jordan. It is six times as salty as the oceans.

106 Asia.

107 The island of Rockall, which is sixteen metres across, rises twenty-three metres out of the Atlantic Ocean and lies some 360 kilometres west of the Outer Hebrides, off Scotland.

108 In Colorado, in the far west of North America.

109 The kangaroo and the emu.

110 Australia.

111 They are belts of light winds and calms where ships became becalmed, a few thousand kilometres north and south of the Equator. They were called horse latitudes by sailors in ships carrying horses. When their ships became becalmed they had to throw the horses overboard because there was not enough fresh water for them.

112 The tropic of Cancer is north of the Equator and the tropic of Capricorn south of it.

113 Australia. It has more than 150,000,000 sheep – nearly fourteen times as many as the people there!

114 A tree whose leaves fall in the autumn (fall). Trees whose leaves don't fall are called evergreen.

115 In the centre and north of Africa.

116 In Asia, north of India.

117 An atlas.

118 When he sailed west across the Atlantic he thought he was sailing towards India because he did not know of the existence of America. When he made land-fall on the islands of the West Indies he thought he had discovered India.

120 *How it works*: It's a bit hard to explain without algebra. The trick depends upon two facts: first, the number you say (5) and the number you put in the envelope (4) add up to 9. Secondly, the audience add your number 5 to their thought number and then take away ten (by crossing off the 1) but then add one on (by putting the 1 beneath their answer). This is the same as taking away 9. You will see how it works if you write out the sums for "thought" numbers 6, 7, 8, 9, and 10 in turn. Each give the number 4.

121 A male silkworm moth can smell a female moth by her scent an amazing eleven kilometres away!

122 Ants keep the little green insects, aphids, which they milk for a sweet juice they exude. We know aphids as the green pests that eat rose leaves.

123 The locust of America.

124 When a bee has found flowers with nectar in them, which bees collect to make honey, he tells the other bees that there are flowers nearby by doing a circular dance. Other bees gather round the dancing bee, then they fly off with him to the flower.

125 A bee can actually tell the other bees in his hive which direction to fly in to get to the flowers. He tells the other bees by doing a circular dance – a sort of eightsome reel in the shape of two half-circles. The other bees can tell from the way he does his dance where the flowers are.

This direction
shows where
the flower is.

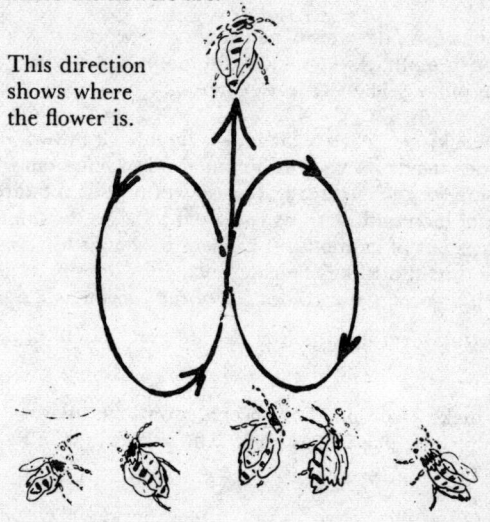

126 Bees buzz their wings to make heat inside the hive. They can also use their wings like fans, to blow air into the hive to cool it in summer.

127 In its legs. It also makes a "chirping" noise by rubbing its legs together. This noise-making is called *stridulating*.

128 A centipede can have a hundred legs, as its name suggests – *centi* means a hundred, *pede* means foot. It may have anything from seventeen to 170 pairs of legs. It is related to the millipede. The word millipede means thousand-footed, but no millipede has been found with that number of feet. Some have been found with 230 pairs of feet. Millipedes can measure as much as twenty-three centimetres.

129 The Mexican fly and the deer bot-fly can both attain a speed of about thirty-eight kilometres an hour.

130 It is a large, greenish, North American insect, like a grasshopper. It gets its name from the male's mating call.

131 A silkworm, despite its name, is not a worm; it is a whitish moth. As you know, all moths come from caterpillars. The silkworm caterpillar makes silk.

132 The silkworm caterpillar makes liquid silk in two glands inside its body. The liquid milk comes out of its mouth in a long thread. The silkworm pulls the thread out of its mouth with its two front legs. As the liquid comes out of its mouth it hardens in the air to a very fine thread of silk. The caterpillar uses the silk to make itself a cocoon and comes out of the cocoon as a moth.

133 The silkworm uses its front feet to pull silk out of its mouth.

134 To make a cocoon. The cocoon covers the silkworm completely, like an egg shell. The silkworm is in its caterpillar stage.

135 The caterpillar changes into a moth inside its cocoon in stages (called instars). It hatches out of the silk cocoon, as a winged moth, after two-to-three weeks.

136 It weighs two tonnes (one tonne plus half two tonnes (its weight) = 1 + 1 = 2 tonnes).

137 43560 or RESIN. Serena should put resin on her bow to make her viola "sing" sweetly.

138 Mercury, Venus, Earth, Mars, Jupiter, Saturn, Uranus, Neptune, Pluto. You can also count the Moon, as the Earth's planet, making ten in all.

139 Venus. It takes about 225 Earth days to revolve all the way round the Sun, but it rotates "clockwise" once in 247 Earth days, that is, about eight months.

140 No it is not a star, it is a planet. Both are names for Venus, the brightest of the planets. It is so bright because it is covered by clouds which reflect light well. It is called the evening star when it appears like a tiny orange light low in the sky in the evening, and the morning star when it appears in the morning.

141 It is a star at a certain stage in its life. All stars start their lives as large and cool; then they shrink and change colour and at first get hotter. They cool down as they get older over millions of years. The Sun is a little older than a white dwarf: it is a yellow dwarf. When it cools down even more, it will become a red dwarf.

142 It is one of millions of galaxies of stars in the universe. You can see it in the night sky as a broad speckled band of stars.

143 The spiral galaxy Andromeda Nebula (which means *cloud*). You can see it with the naked eye in the Milky Way as a faint haze.

144 **a** The Plough **b** Cassiopeia **c** The Little Bear

145 The sun is about 6000°C, which is about twice as hot as a cigarette, which is 3000°C.

146 A light year is the distance that light travels in a year. It is a distance, not a period of time. Light travels at 300,000 kilometres per second, so a light year is nearly 10,000,000 kilometres. The sun is just over eight light years from the earth. It takes just over eight minutes for light to travel from the sun to the earth.

147 *Proxima Centauri.* It is just over four-and-a-quarter light years away, or over 40,000,000 kilometres away. So it takes light over four years and three months to reach earth.

148 If two of the letters went in the right envelopes, then the third must also have gone into the right envelope! So it's a certainty.

149 Don't move the coins shown shaded.
Move the three coins shown
dashed to their new positions.
Now you have a triangle pointing
downards.

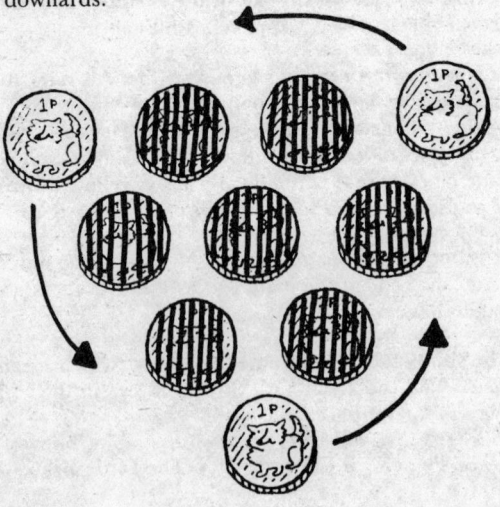

150   285714
              x3
            857142

151 It means *terrible lizard*.

152 The giant twenty-four metre *Brontosaurus* was the
largest land-dwelling animal ever. It ate a tonne of
vegetation per day, and weighed fifty tonnes. It was
more than thirteen metres tall.

153 *Tyrannosaurus Rex*. It was the largest meat-eating
animal that ever lived. It measured about fifteen
metres from head to tail, stood six metres high on its
hind legs, and had a head over a metre long. It had
fifteen-centimetre-long teeth, which were cruelly sharp.
Although it had small useless front legs, it ate smaller
dinosaurs.

154 The rattlesnake can tell where the rabbit is by the warmth or heat it gives out. The snake has a special "eye" that senses heat (not light). This "eye" can pick up the faintest heat rays just as our eyes can pick up light rays. Remember, the desert is cold at night so a warm rabbit would "stand out" against the cold background of the sand.

155 The most venomous snake is probably the tiny krait from Java, or possibly the beak sea snake found in the Pacific Ocean.

156 The tuatara, a brownish lizard-like creature that lives on the rocky islands off the coast of New Zealand. It closely resembles its ancestors of a million years ago.

157 It is the largest lizard in the world, as much as five metres long. It is a green monitor lizard; it is not a dragon! The Komodo Dragon is very fierce and uses its teeth to attack it prey – small mammals, birds and lizards – and lashes its tail like a whip. It is found only on the small islands in Indonesia, including the island of Komodo from which it gets its name.

158 South American bullfrog.

159 It is actually a lizard though it looks like a snake. Its legs are inside its body and do not show.

160 Eight balls in the box.

162 If her clock weren't fast, it would be five o'clock because it chimes two strokes more than the hour. But the clock is half-an-hour fast, so the correct time is half-past four.

163 They washed themselves with olive-oil, earth, or plant ashes. They also rubbed themselves with bran, sand and pumice-stone.

164 Soap-making began by accident about 3000 years ago on Sapo Hill in Rome. Animals were sacrificed on the hill and mixed with ashes from the altar fires. The mixture ran downhill to the banks of the Tiber river, where it formed a slippery clay. Washerwomen on the banks found that when they pounded clothes into the clay the clothes became cleaner than usual. Out of this clay came soap.

165 For reds they had cochineal – the food colouring you use to make white icing pink; yellows and greens came from plants, but they faded after a time and were not as bright as modern chemical dye colours; blue came from indigo, a blue dye made in India from the Indigo plant.

166 Nearly two metres.

167 *c* Greek, *d* Henry V, *a* Queen Elizabeth I, *b* Queen Victoria.

168 About one centimetre every hundred days, or about one millimetre in ten days.

169 About twelve centimetres a year.

170 It is a condition of the eye that makes part of what we see – but only part – blurred. So a person suffering from astigmatism, looking at a clock, might see some of the numbers perfectly clearly but some others blurred. One eye may be more astigmatic than the other. Lenses are needed to correct astigmatism.

171 Silk is made at silk farms. Silkworm cocoons are dipped in hot water. This quickly kills the moth inside. Then the long silk thread is unravelled from the cocoon. This is done first by hand then by machine. A cocoon may have up to one kilometre of silk in it! Silk is very, very strong. Ten threads of silk spun together are so strong it is hard to snap them with your hands. At the mill the silk thread is woven into silk cloth.

You can test your own eyes *very roughly* by looking at this pattern. If some of the lines look darker or lighter than others then one of your eyes may be astigmatic. But don't rely on this test. This is just for fun!

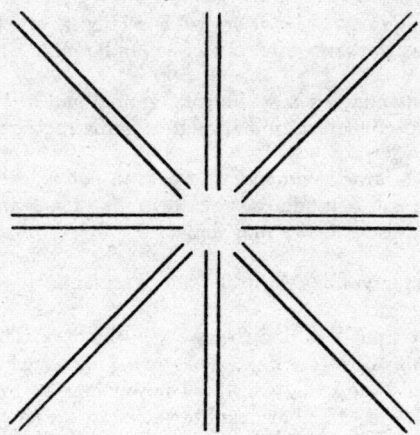

172 Five hippos; six grey animals; ten animals.

173 Only 3 is correct, the other should be:
1. 92, **2.** 35, **4.** 26, **5.** 28, **6.** 69.

174 An African elephant has smaller ears than an Indian elephant. The African elephant cannot be tamed as an Indian elephant can.

175 The rhino with two horns comes from Africa; the rhino with one horn comes from India.

176 He uses his tusks for fighting. He also uses them to shift heavy trees that are in his way. And, most surprising of all, he uses them to dig into the ground for salt. He then scoops up the salty earth with his trunk and puts it into his mouth. For elephants, like you and me, need salt.

177 Apes use stalks of grass to fish out termites from the earth. They break off a stalk and poke it into termite hills. Termites are not ants, but they look like them. Apes use the stalk as you or I use a stick to prod something. This means apes can use tools, like man.

178 The hyrax, believe it or not, is related to an elephant! It has the same kind of feet as jumbo has.

179 The panda is a most unusual animal and it is not a bear: its nearest animal relative is the raccoon.

180 It is a large salamander. It lives in ponds in North America. A mudlark is an Australian black-and-white bird, also called a magpie lark.

181 The platypus of Australia and Tasmania.

182 They squeak to find their way in the dark. They cannot see in the dark. They make high-pitched sounds like a dog whistle. The sounds echo from trees and walls. The bat hears the echoes with its enormous ears. The bat "sees" where it is going with its ears just as you or I see with our eyes.

183 Ostriches roam the African grasslands in groups. When their young are hatched, the mothers herd them together in a *crèche*, guarded by the father ostriches. (The word crèche comes from the French word meaning a crib for babies: you say it '*craysh*'.) When the fathers of two crèches of young ostriches meet, the fathers of the two groups do an extraordinary dance. When this is over, the two groups can accept one another and they combine their two crèches to make one big flock. This is what is known as crèching.

184 The giraffe, whose neck is so long it stands about 5.5 metres tall.

185 The cheetah of Africa.

186 It is a large sea animal, a mammal. It lives in the Indian Ocean, the Red Sea, and the waters round Australia. It looks like a whale with its snub nose, flippers, long body and forked tail. It is hunted, alas, for its blubber, used as a kind of cod-liver oil.

187 An oyster lays the most – as many as 5,000,000,000 eggs in a year, then a sturgeon with 7,000,000 eggs and a toad with a mere 6000 eggs.

188 The tortoise lives the longest. One common box tortoise lived to 138 years of age.

189 A Bactrian camel has two humps and a dromedary is a camel with one hump.

190 The eagle is a bird with wings; the other animals are not birds, they are mammals.

191 **a** hedgehog **b** red deer **c** fox **d** wolf
e horse **f** hare **g** rat **h** rabbit
i otter **j** badger

192 Couldn't you see a Dalmatian dog?

193 Seven hippos (giving twenty-eight legs) and nine ostriches (eighteen legs), making forty-six legs in all.

194 She can pop the egg in a bowl of water. If it sinks, it is good and fresh; if it floats, it is not fresh, and may even be bad.

195

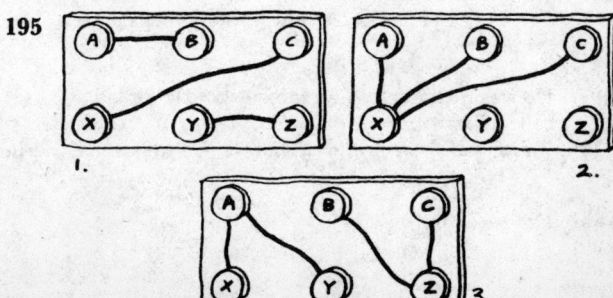

87

196 It weighs more. You can try it with a real cup of water and a cork.

197 Surprise, surprise! Both tins should get to the bottom of the slope together. Tins of all sizes roll at the same speed. Isn't science marvellous?

199 Thirty kilos.

200 Did you see a knight on a horse?

201 Thirty-seven plays, the most famous of which is *Hamlet*. Other well-known ones are *The Merchant of Venice*, *A Midsummer Night's Dream* and *The Tempest*.

202 Geoffrey Chaucer. It is a collection of stories written in verse, in olde English. It was first printed by William Caxton in 1478.

203 The Chinese printed books from type made of baked clay in 1000BC or thereabouts. But their type was not moveable. One of the first books printed from moveable type was the Bible by Johannes Gutenberg at Mainz in Germany in 1456. It became known as the Gutenberg Bible. There are still some forty copies in existence, and each is worth a small fortune.

204 He was one of the pioneers of printing and he published the first printed books in England in 1477.

205 He was aptly named, because he was Caxton's foreman, and like Caxton he was another pioneer printer.

207 He was a character in a famous booklet of tall stories called *Baron Munchausen's Narrative of His Marvellous Travels and Campaigns in Russia*. It was first published in

Britain in 1785. The author was probably Rudolph Erich Raspe, a German who lived in London. There was a real Baron Munchausen who lived in Germany in the 1700s. He died of grief at being thought of as the biggest boaster in the world; actually, he was a perfectly ordinary man. The name is still used to describe a boaster, a teller of tall stories. One of the Baron's fantastic adventures tells how he flew across the River Thames on a cannon ball. He was sleeping in a charged cannon when someone fired it and he sailed across the Thames as a shot out of a cannon.

208 Also known as *The Thousand and One Nights*, it is a storybook of fantasy about such characters as Aladdin, Ali Baba and Sinbad the Sailor.

209 She appears as the main character in the storybook *Arabian Nights*. In the main story of this book the Sultan Shahriyar decreed that each girl he married would be put to death the morning after the wedding. Scheherazade, the daughter of the grand vizier, offered to marry him if he would allow her to tell him just one story. She stopped her story at the most exciting point. The Sultan became so interested that he allowed her to live another day so she could finish the story. She then began another tale and she continued to tell stories for a thousand and one nights, by which time the Sultan had fallen in love with her and did not put her to death.

210 The lead costs £1, the collar £2.

211 The ten plagues were: The Nile waters turned to blood; a plague of frogs; a plague of gnats; a plague of flies; cattle disease; a plague of boils; hail and thunder; a plague of locusts; three days of darkness; all the first-born children were killed.

212 A Dutch lens-maker, Hans Lippershey, in 1608. But most people think Galileo did. He made a telescope in 1610 which was much better than Lippershey's. He also made the instrument world-famous.

213 Alexander Graham Bell, an American inventor, in 1876.

214 An Italian engineer, Guglielmo Marconi, in the early 1900s. The radio was originally called the 'wireless' because it did not need wires to transmit the radio programmes.

215 They all helped to invent the petrol-driven motor car.

216 The Wright brothers, Orville and Wilbur, made their historic flight at Kitty Hawk, North Carolina, on December 17, 1903. The two brothers built their petrol-engined biplane, of flimsy cloth, wood and wires. Orville made the first flight which was 36.5 metres long.

217 John Boyd Dunlop, a Scottish veterinary surgeon, fitted the first pneumatic tyre to a bicycle in 1888.

218 Penny-farthing bicycles had front wheels up to 132 cm in diameter. They had pedals but no gears. The first one was built in 1870.

219 They were all names of early kinds of bicycle. The célérifére and vélocifére were French, made in the early 1800s; the Draisenne was the German version of the English hobby-horse or dandy-horse; later two-wheeled bicycles were called bone-shakers.

220 Leonardo da Vinci, the Italian painter. He was not only one of the greatest painters ever, he was a great inventor. Unfortunately, he never had the time or the materials to build his submarine. But his drawings show clearly how it would have worked.

221 Robert Wilhelm Bunsen (1811–1899), a German chemist. Bunsen burners are used in most school laboratories.

222 You probably thought it was George Stephenson. He made the first railway engine that could pull carriages along a railway line. But the real inventor of the railway engine was Richard Trevithick, a Cornishman. His engine showed that a steam engine was a practical possibility.

223 Margarine is a manufactured mixture of fats and oils. It is cheaper than butter. It was invented by a French chemist Hippolyte Mège Mourries. He churned together beef oleo oil, milk, water and *annatto*, a bright orange vegetable dye.

225

5	9	14
4	10	14
9	19	28

8	7	15
9	11	20
17	18	35

13	5	18
10	12	22
23	17	40

11	12	23
13	14	27
24	26	50

227

228 1 mile, 2 moss, 3 cry, 4 home, 5 valour, 6 chickens,
hatched, 7 fire, 8 worm, 9 mice, 10 gander, 11 mind.

229

D	U	S	T
D	U	S	K
T	U	S	K
T	A	S	K
T	A	N	K

B	A	S	K
B	A	R	K
D	A	R	K
D	A	R	T
D	I	R	T

L	A	N	E
L	O	N	E
L	O	S	E
L	O	S	T
P	O	S	T

P	I	G
W	I	G
W	A	G
W	A	Y
S	A	Y
S	T	Y

230

1 toves	8 soup
2 wabe	9 ladles
3 mimsy	10 day
4 outgrabe	11 tree
5 cats	12 Piggy-wig
6 babies	13 nose
7 vats	

231

232 authoress, duchess, empress, heiress, hostess,
manageress, goddess, tigress, *marchioness, *countess,
*lass, *witch.